THE REFINED POET PRESENTS

Poetry Anthology Series

Sanctuary for the Soul
*
A Poetical Anthology for Life's Journey

Written by: The Refined Poet

Sanctuary for the Soul
A Poetical Anthology for Life's Journey

All Rights reserved ©2012 by The Refined Poet

No part of this book may be reproduced or transmitted in any form or by any means, graphic, electronic, or mechanical, including photocopying, recording, taping, or by any information storage or retrieval system, without the permission in writing from the publisher.

Front & Back Cover Designs by Abundant Truth Publishing
Image by Ruslan Sikunov from Pixabay

Abundant Truth Publishing
an imprint of Abundant Truth International Ministries

For information address:
Abundant Truth International
P.O. Box 126
Camden, NC 27921

Unless otherwise indicated, all of the scripture quotations are taken from the *Authorized King James Version* **of the Bible. Scripture quotations marked with NIV are taken from the** *New International Version* **of the Bible. Scripture quotations marked with ASV are taken from the** *American Standard Version* **of the Bible. Scripture quotations marked with GW are taken from the** *God's Word Bible.*

ISBN 13: 978-1-60141-217-1

Printed in the United States of America.

Contents

Preface

Introduction

Section 1 - Comforted by the Creator   1

Peace   *3*
Grace   *7*
All Because   *11*

Section 2 - Walking with Christ   15

Midnight Madness   *17*
'Tis the Night   *21*
Worth It All   *25*

Section 3 – Created to Worship and Praise   29

Call His Name   *31*
Love   *35*
Hope   *39*

Section 4 – Faithful Creator   43

Beauty for Ashes   *45*

Contents *(cont.)*

The Comforter   *49*
Silent Cry   *53*

Just for Fun   **57**

Walking   *59*

About the Author   **61**

My Poetic Offerings   **63**

Preface

I hope the poems of this anthology will encourage and inspire. I create poetry under the pseudonym of "The Refined Poet" due to the style of my writings.

I do not write from a place of angst, frustration, or inner turmoil. My poetry comes from biblical, thoughtful introspection and consideration of various topics while respecting the many forms of the poetic genre. Hope you enjoy this collection. – TRP

Introduction

Everyone needs a place of rest. Since life never stops, true rest can only be found inwardly. The poems in this anthology are crafted to encourage those of the Christian faith. In addition, the poetic pieces will inspire all those who appreciate the poetry genre.

SANCTUARY FOR THE SOUL

A Poetical Anthology for Life's Journey

-SECION 1-

~Comforted by the Creator~
(Poems Reflecting God's Care in Life's Journey)

SANCTUARY FOR THE SOUL
A Poetical Anthology for Life's Journey

Scripture: And let the peace of God rule in your hearts, to the which also ye are called in one body; and be ye thankful. - Colossians 3:15

Inspiration: *This poetic piece encourages us to walk in the peace of God daily. Challenges will come, but we must allow His promises and presence in our lives to give us peace.*
~TRP~

SANCTUARY FOR THE SOUL

A Poetical Anthology for Life's Journey

~*Peace*~
(Englyn Milwr Style)

The Eternal One abides,

Under His wings you can hide.

Shun all cares, the heavy tides.

Men buckle under life's trials.

Forgetting the Place on high,

Where the Holy One resides.

Run to Him with tears in eyes,

Trust He won't turn you aside.

Bringing peace to the heart's cry.

SANCTUARY FOR THE SOUL
A Poetical Anthology for Life's Journey

My Reflections

SANCTUARY FOR THE SOUL
A Poetical Anthology for Life's Journey

My Reflections

SANCTUARY FOR THE SOUL
A Poetical Anthology for Life's Journey

Scripture: But by the grace of God I am what I am: and his grace which was bestowed upon me was not in vain; but I laboured more abundantly than they all: yet not I, but the grace of God which was with me. – I Corinthians 15:10

Inspiration: This poetic piece was written after having a "I Thank God for grace moment." All of what we have received from Christ is through grace. If we accomplish any great work, service, or ministry, it is because of His grace working through us. We don't have to earn it or work for it, just accept it. ~TRP~

SANCTUARY FOR THE SOUL

A Poetical Anthology for Life's Journey

~*Grace*~
(Monorhyme Style)

What can be said of God's grace?

Is it found in a certain place?

Though no one has seen His face,

You can know He exists by faith.

Faith helps you to run the race,

Grace keeps you striving in pace.

We may not always realize the stakes,

We must not lose hope after mistakes.

Remembering His love is never fake,

Lift your head and thank Him for grace.

SANCTUARY FOR THE SOUL
A Poetical Anthology for Life's Journey

My Reflections

SANCTUARY FOR THE SOUL
A Poetical Anthology for Life's Journey

My Reflections

SANCTUARY FOR THE SOUL
A Poetical Anthology for Life's Journey

Scripture: And let the peace of God rule in your hearts, to the which also ye are called in one body; and be ye thankful. - Colossians 3:15

Inspiration: *This poetic piece encourages us to walk in the peace of God daily. Challenges will come, but we must allow His promises and presence in our lives to give us peace.*
~TRP~

SANCTUARY FOR THE SOUL
A Poetical Anthology for Life's Journey

~*All Because*~
(ABC Style)

A ll because of His love

B e strong and of good courage

C ontinue to stand in hard times

D elving into your destiny

E xpecting pain to become purpose

F oreseeing future success and fulfillment

G oing from this life into the next in peace

SANCTUARY FOR THE SOUL
A Poetical Anthology for Life's Journey

My Reflections

_____

_____

_____

_____

_____

_____

_____

_____

_____

_____

_____

_____

_____

_____

SANCTUARY FOR THE SOUL
A Poetical Anthology for Life's Journey

My Reflections

SANCTUARY FOR THE SOUL
A Poetical Anthology for Life's Journey

SANCTUARY FOR THE SOUL
A Poetical Anthology for Life's Journey

-Section 2-
~Walking with Christ~
(Poems concerning the Daily Toils of Life's Journey)

SANCTUARY FOR THE SOUL
A Poetical Anthology for Life's Journey

Scripture: ...Weeping may endure for a night, but joy cometh in the morning. – Psalm 30:5

Inspiration: *This poetic piece describes angst we can feel when left alone with our thoughts at night; rejoicing in God's faithfulness. ~TRP~*

SANCTUARY FOR THE SOUL
A Poetical Anthology for Life's Journey

~*Midnight Madness*~

Somewhere between morning and night
Dwells the awesome minute called midnight.
Troubles of one day stand to challenge the next,
While thoughts of rest, sometimes, don't refresh.

Hopes that the dawning of a new day
Will bring hope and peace,
Midnight madness makes it seem bleak.

Will it be better?
Will it be worse?
Midnight madness is certainly a curse!

Well in a moment these thoughts come as flashes,
For only a minute lasts the midnight madness.

Then words of hope and faith spring into my mind.
The words of the psalm stand up just in time.

Reminding me of the faithfulness of the Creator;
He who is the Ultimate Motivator.

The midnight madness passes with the psalmist's words spawning,
"Weeping may endure for a night, but joy comes in the morning."

SANCTUARY FOR THE SOUL
A Poetical Anthology for Life's Journey

My Reflections

SANCTUARY FOR THE SOUL
A Poetical Anthology for Life's Journey

Scripture: Being confident of this very thing, that he which hath begun a good work in you will perform it until the day of Jesus Christ. - Philippians 1:6

Inspiration: *This poetic piece describes anticipation that we all feel when embarking on new endeavors; the Christian remains confident because of Christ's presence. ~TRP~*

SANCTUARY FOR THE SOUL

A Poetical Anthology for Life's Journey

~'Tis the Night~
(Tritina Style)

'Tis the night before my new life begins.

What will happen as the new day emerges,

Fear, regret, or earnest expectations?

"Nothing ventured, nothing gained:"

or just futile expectations,

While a scenario of possible failure begins.

Through the clutter of thoughts, hope emerges.

Confidence of a bright future emerges,

Making me a slave to raised expectations.

A smirk, a smile, a new expression on my face begins.

SANCTUARY FOR THE SOUL
A Poetical Anthology for Life's Journey

My new life begins, emerges, with glorious expectations.

SANCTUARY FOR THE SOUL
A Poetical Anthology for Life's Journey

My Reflections

_____

_____

_____

_____

_____

_____

_____

_____

_____

_____

_____

_____

_____

_____

_____

_____

SANCTUARY FOR THE SOUL
A Poetical Anthology for Life's Journey

Scripture: For our light affliction, which is but for a moment, worketh for us a far more exceeding and eternal weight of glory. – 2 Corinthians 4:17

Inspiration: *This poetic piece reflects on one's walk with Christ with its many ups and downs; looking forward to the eternal reward of heaven. ~TRP~*

SANCTUARY FOR THE SOUL

A Poetical Anthology for Life's Journey

~*Worth It All*~

"I will never leave you;
I will never forsake you."
These words of Christ are true,
Even when life deals its worst to you.

One thing is certain,
and two things are true.
The love of God is amazing;
He'll always be there for you.

Pain upon pain.
Sadness and despair.
Hurt beyond hurt.
These do not diminish the worth.

The worth of knowing God.
The joy of walking with Him,

SANCTUARY FOR THE SOUL
A Poetical Anthology for Life's Journey

Even when all seems dim.
Hope remains for strength in this life
And in the life to come.

It will be worth it all when He opens His arms.
And say in that day of days,
"Welcome home my servant, well done!"

SANCTUARY FOR THE SOUL
A Poetical Anthology for Life's Journey

My Reflections

SANCTUARY FOR THE SOUL
A Poetical Anthology for Life's Journey

SANCTUARY FOR THE SOUL
A Poetical Anthology for Life's Journey

-Section 3-
~Created to Worship and Praise~
(Poems Declaring His Praises Life's Journey)

SANCTUARY FOR THE SOUL
A Poetical Anthology for Life's Journey

Scripture: And in that day shall ye say, Praise the LORD, call upon his name, declare his doings among the people, make mention that his name is exalted. - Isaiah 12:4

Inspiration: *This poetic piece challenges us to call upon the name of the Lord and declare His goodness. We must always remember His kindness towards us, demonstrated in Christ's sacrifice. ~TRP~*

SANCTUARY FOR THE SOUL
A Poetical Anthology for Life's Journey

~Call His Name~

Call upon the name of the Lord

Oh you who believe in Him.

He will cover you with peace

His favor and kindness will guide thee

There is no want to those who trust Him.

Make known His works!

Declare His wonderful acts.

Great is the Lord God

And power be to His Anointed One.

Praise the Lord,

At the remembrance of His name.

SANCTUARY FOR THE SOUL
A Poetical Anthology for Life's Journey

My Reflections

_____

_____

_____

_____

_____

_____

_____

_____

_____

_____

_____

_____

_____

_____

SANCTUARY FOR THE SOUL
A Poetical Anthology for Life's Journey

My Reflections

_____

_____

_____

_____

_____

_____

_____

_____

_____

_____

_____

_____

_____

_____

_____

SANCTUARY FOR THE SOUL
A Poetical Anthology for Life's Journey

Scripture: A Psalm of David, the servant of the LORD, who spake unto the LORD the words of this song in the day that the LORD delivered him from the hand of all his enemies, and from the hand of Saul: And he said, I will love thee, O LORD, my strength. – Psalm 18:1

Inspiration: *This poetic piece expresses love and appreciation for God and His wonderful works. The Christian must remain mindful, grateful, and express love towards Him.*
~TRP~

SANCTUARY FOR THE SOUL
A Poetical Anthology for Life's Journey

~Love~

I love the Lord

He heard my cry.

When troubles arise

He comforts me in the night.

Therefore, will I praise Him.

I must glorify Him

And bless His holy name.

My soul magnifies the Lord

My heart longs for Him

So, I will seek Him.

SANCTUARY FOR THE SOUL
A Poetical Anthology for Life's Journey

My Reflections

SANCTUARY FOR THE SOUL
A Poetical Anthology for Life's Journey

My Reflections

SANCTUARY FOR THE SOUL
A Poetical Anthology for Life's Journey

Scripture: And hope maketh not ashamed; because the love of God is shed abroad in our hearts by the Holy Ghost which is given unto us. - Romans 5:5

Inspiration: *Senryu reflecting the attributes of hope. The Christian's hope is rooted in faith in Christ. Our hope helps us to persevere through trials and tests looking for the true Blessed Hope. ~TRP~*

SANCTUARY FOR THE SOUL
A Poetical Anthology for Life's Journey

~*Hope*~

...A Senyru

Raises Expectations

Overlooks the obstacles

Receives in Patience

SANCTUARY FOR THE SOUL
A Poetical Anthology for Life's Journey

My Reflections

SANCTUARY FOR THE SOUL
A Poetical Anthology for Life's Journey

My Reflections

SANCTUARY FOR THE SOUL
A Poetical Anthology for Life's Journey

SANCTUARY FOR THE SOUL
A Poetical Anthology for Life's Journey

-Section 4-
~Faithful Creator~
(Poems Declaring His Faithfulness as Lord of All)

SANCTUARY FOR THE SOUL
A Poetical Anthology for Life's Journey

Scripture: *"To appoint unto them that mourn in Zion, to give unto them beauty for ashes, the oil of joy for mourning, the garment of praise for the spirit of heaviness; that they might be called trees of righteousness, the planting of the LORD, that he might be glorified." – Isaiah 61:3*

Inspiration: *This poetic piece reflects how Christ came work all things in our lives for good. He can turn adverse circumstances into beautiful testimonies of His goodness and grace. ~TRP~*

SANCTUARY FOR THE SOUL

A Poetical Anthology for Life's Journey

~Beauty for Ashes~

What can be said of the joy you bring?

I once was mute, now my heart sings.

You have filled the very void of my soul.

With hope and gladness, you have made me whole.

A weathered being from life's stinging lashes,

My life is now complete, receiving beauty for ashes.

SANCTUARY FOR THE SOUL
A Poetical Anthology for Life's Journey

My Poetic Prose

SANCTUARY FOR THE SOUL
A Poetical Anthology for Life's Journey

My Poetic Prose

SANCTUARY FOR THE SOUL
A Poetical Anthology for Life's Journey

Scripture: For the kingdom of God is.... righteousness, and peace, and joy in the Holy Ghost - Romans 14:17

Inspiration: *Poem appreciating the Holy Spirit's work in my Christian life. He reveals to us the love and faithfulness of God and of Christ. He reminds us that we are not alone and that heaven will be with us. ~TRP ~*

SANCTUARY FOR THE SOUL

A Poetical Anthology for Life's Journey

~*The Comforter*~
(Romans 14:17)

Your presence radiates, resonates with peace and power.

The joy you bring floods my hungry soul.

Your Word calms my thoughts and soothes my mind.

You reveal the Father's love and the Son's comfort.

Bestowing abundant inspiration and consolation

The Comforter, you are to me.

SANCTUARY FOR THE SOUL
A Poetical Anthology for Life's Journey

My Poetic Prose

SANCTUARY FOR THE SOUL
A Poetical Anthology for Life's Journey

My Poetic Prose

SANCTUARY FOR THE SOUL
A Poetical Anthology for Life's Journey

Scripture: When my father and my mother forsake me, then the LORD will take me up. Psalm 27:10

Inspiration: *Poem describing loneliness and despair that one may feel. Though this experience occurs, the Christian must know that when no one seems to care or understand, the Lord is always present and will answer. ~TRP~*

SANCTUARY FOR THE SOUL
A Poetical Anthology for Life's Journey

~*Silent Cry*~

I cry

No one hears

I call

No one cares

I weep

No one sees

I ask

No one helps

I plead

No one feels

I beg

No one gives

I sleep

Rest flees from me

SANCTUARY FOR THE SOUL
A Poetical Anthology for Life's Journey

I eat

Foods don't satisfy me

I weep

Tears escape me

No one hears

No one cares

No one sees

My silent cry

SANCTUARY FOR THE SOUL
A Poetical Anthology for Life's Journey

My Poetic Prose

SANCTUARY FOR THE SOUL
A Poetical Anthology for Life's Journey

SANCTUARY FOR THE SOUL
A Poetical Anthology for Life's Journey

Just for Fun

SANCTUARY FOR THE SOUL
A Poetical Anthology for Life's Journey

Inspiration: *Poem written for personal enjoyment. Hope you like it. ~TRP~*

SANCTUARY FOR THE SOUL

A Poetical Anthology for Life's Journey

~*Walking*~

Flip-flop goes my shoes

As I walk the side of the pool

Click-clack goes my clods

As I walk the shops of the mall

Stomp-stomp goes my boots

As I fall, giving everyone a hoot.

SANCTUARY FOR THE SOUL
A Poetical Anthology for Life's Journey

My Poetic Prose

SANCTUARY FOR THE SOUL
A Poetical Anthology for Life's Journey

~*About the Author*~

The Refined Poet is a poet, psalmist, author, and minister. He has written numerous poems, books, articles, blogs, teaching resources, devotional materials, and music for the Christian community.

His poetry reflects sound, biblical Christian thought, encouraging those of the Christian faith. His versatility in poetic prose provides inspiration for those who appreciate the poetry genre. His motto for his poetry is: "Write to Inspire. Write to Express. Write to Live."

I create poetry under the pseudonym of "The Refined Poet" due to the style of my writings. I do not write from a place of angst, frustration, or inner turmoil. My poetry comes from biblical, thoughtful introspection and consideration of various topics while respecting the many forms of the poetic genre. ~TRP~

SANCTUARY FOR THE SOUL
A Poetical Anthology for Life's Journey

For more poetry, please visit The Refined Poet online at therefinedpoet.net

SANCTUARY FOR THE SOUL
A Poetical Anthology for Life's Journey

My Poetic Offerings

SANCTUARY FOR THE SOUL
A Poetical Anthology for Life's Journey

"In this section, I invite you to try creating some poetry of your own."

SANCTUARY FOR THE SOUL
A Poetical Anthology for Life's Journey

My Poetic Prose

SANCTUARY FOR THE SOUL
A Poetical Anthology for Life's Journey

My Poetic Prose

SANCTUARY FOR THE SOUL
A Poetical Anthology for Life's Journey

My Poetic Prose

SANCTUARY FOR THE SOUL
A Poetical Anthology for Life's Journey

My Poetic Prose

SANCTUARY FOR THE SOUL
A Poetical Anthology for Life's Journey

My Poetic Prose

SANCTUARY FOR THE SOUL
A Poetical Anthology for Life's Journey

y Poetic Prose

SANCTUARY FOR THE SOUL
A Poetical Anthology for Life's Journey

My Poetic Prose

SANCTUARY FOR THE SOUL
A Poetical Anthology for Life's Journey

My Poetic Prose

www.ingramcontent.com/pod-product-compliance
Lightning Source LLC
Chambersburg PA
CBHW050343010526
44119CB00049B/682